I0069867

Lee Lister is a Business Consultant with more than 25 year's consultancy experience for many household names. On the internet, she is known as The Bid Manager or The Biz Guru.

From an early age, she began an unparalleled journey through business consulting that continues to span across the UK, USA, Europe and Asia. She has consulted for many companies all over the world. Specialising in business change management, start up consultancy and trouble shooting. She is highly skilled in seminars, lectures and corporate presentations on business, project management and bid management. Lee's experience in marketing and internet marketing is also keenly sought after.

She is a prolific published writer of books, ebooks and articles on business, entrepreneurship and bid management. She can be found easily on major search engines and Amazon.

Lee owns and manages three career based web sites: www.JobSuccess.co.uk   www.WriteCVs.com   and www.ResumeGuys.com

First published in Great Britain in 2008. Previous incarnations were sold as ebooks from 2002.

ISBN: 978-1-907551-03-1

Other books available include:
Proposal Writing For Smaller Businesses
Consultants' Tool Box
Profitable New Quilting Business
Profitable New Face Painting Business
Profitable New Bottled Water Business
Profitable New T Shirt Printing Business
Profitable New Cake Decoration Business
Profitable New Manicurist Business

FastTrack© To Job Success

www.JobSuccess.co.uk

This book is dedicated to my daughter Kerry Lister for whom I have always strived to be my best.

CONTENTS

Legal Notice -- **10**

Introduction --- **11**

Writing Your C.V. _____ *13*

C.V. Writing-- **14**

Chronological C.V. ------------------------------------- 15

Functional C.V. --- 15

Student C.V. -- 17

Professional C.V. --------------------------------------- 17

Headers and Footers------------------------------- 18

Your Name and Contact Details --------------------- 18

Career Overview or Personal Statement ------------ 19

Qualifications-- 20

Technical Skills-------------------------------------- 21

Career Experience ---------------------------------- 22

Key Achievements ---------------------------------- 22

Key Skills-- 23

Relevant Experience -------------------------------- 23

Personal Achievements ----------------------------- 23

Design of Your C.V. --------------------------------- 23

Cover Letter--- 24

Cover Letter Tips-------------------------------------- 26

C.V. Check List --------------------------------------- 28

Tips On Writing Your C.V. --------------------------- **29**

Students and Recent Graduates. -------------------- 31

For New Graduates. --------------------------------- 32

Sales Staff -- 32

IT Staff -- 32

Senior Manager --- 32

Professors, Medical etc ------------------------------------- 33

Company Application Forms------------------------------- 33

A Lesson in Bad C.V. Writing ----------------------- **34**

Where do I begin - It looks awful! --------------------- 39

Weaknesses On Your C.V. ------------------------------ **41**

Gaps in Work History ----------------------------------- 41

Being Out of Work --------------------------------------- 41

Changing Careers -- 42

Negatives in your Work History --------------------- 43

Unrelated Job History ---------------------------------- 44

Recent Graduate --- 44

Too Little Experience ----------------------------------- 45

Over Qualified-- 46

Not Sure of Job Objective ----------------------------- 47

Less Education than Normally Required -------------- 47

Major C.V. Writing Errors ---------------------------- **48**

Structure Of Your C.V.---------------------------------- 48

Design -- 50

Contents-- 53

C.V. Blunders --- **57**

Typos and Grammar Slips ------------------------------ 57

Bad Humour-- 58

Sample C.V.'s-- **60**

Job Searching Strategies _____ **67**

Introduction --- **68**

Steps In Your Job Campaign --------------------------- 68

Not Sure What You Want To Do? --------------------- 70

Not Been Working For Some Time. -------------------- 72

Your Career In A Changing Economy ------------------ 73

Networking --- 75

Whom Should I Try To Meet? ------------------------- 75

Self Marketing-- 77

Ethical Issues --- 79

Job Searching and Technology ---------------------- 80

Should I send my C.V. off on Spec? ------------------- 81

Applying Online --- 82

Your Web Personae And Your C.V. -------------------- 83

Job Fairs --- 84

Your Job Search Plan ---------------------------------- 88

Interview Techniques _____ **90**

Interview Preparation--------------------------------- 91

Nine Steps To Perfect Preparation ------------------ 94

Frequently Asked Questions -------------------------- 96

Interview Tips--102

The 5-Rule Interview Plan ---------------------------108

Rule 1: Positive At All Times ------------------------- 108

Rule 2: Quantitative v Qualitative ------------------- 109

Rule 3: No Misunderstandings ----------------------- 110

Rule 4: Keeping To The Point ------------------------ 111

Rule 5: Be Positive------------------------------------- 112

The Day of the Interview ----------------------------114

Preparing Employer Questions ----------------------117

Five Questions They'll Love... ----------------------119

And Five They will Hate! ----------------------------120

Job Offers--121

Evaluating Your Job Offer ------------------------------ 122

Follow Up Visits -- 122

Negotiating Your Salary Package ------------------124

Action Phrases and Power Verbs--------------------126

Action Phrases --- 126

Power Verbs-- 127

Tables:

TABLE 1: CHRONOLOGICAL C.V. TEMPLATE 15

TABLE 2: FUNCTIONAL C.V. TEMPLATE 16

TABLE 3: STUDENT C.V. TEMPLATE..17

Legal Notice

We do not believe in get rich quick schemes. We do believe that success is equal parts of inspiration, hard work and luck. Every effort has been made to represent accurately our product and it is potential.

Please remember that each individual's success depends on his or her background, dedication, desire, and motivation. As with any endeavour, there is an inherent risk of loss of capital. **There is no guarantee that you will earn any money or obtain a new job**.

This book will provide you with a number of suggestions you can use to aid your chances for success. **We do not and cannot guarantee any level of success.**

This book is written with the warning that any and every venture contains risks, and any number of alternatives. We do not suggest that any one way is the right way or that our suggestions are the only way.

Introduction

This book, written by the owner of probably the best C.V. and interview services website in the UK www.jobsuccess.co.uk details all you need to know to **Get the Job you Deserve!**

Are you a fresh graduate and planning to look for a job? Did you just recently quit your job and are looking for greener pastures? Are you unemployed and have little experience regarding ways to secure a job? Whatever your situation may, be this is the book for you.

With the current slow down in the world economy, more and more people are seeking that competitive advantage in a very challenging environment. Remember:

Your job is to find a job

This is the most important advice that I can give you. Tempting as it may be to have a few lie in's, drown your sorrows or have that break you promised yourself when you were working hard. Now is not the time. If you want to find the great job that you deserve then you must teat finding the next job seriously.

Sit down and make yourself up a To Do List, schedule or work plan – however you work best and decide for how ever long it takes (hopefully not too long) your job will be to find your next step on your career ladder.

I am going to take you through the following:
- Your C.V.
- Your Job Searching Strategy.
- Your Interview Strategy.

For ease of use, I will tend to use the word C.V. to mean either a C.V. or Resume – the same object just given a different name depending upon in which country you are seeking work.

So I wish you luck in the search for the

Job You Deserve!

Writing Your C.V.

C.V. Writing

For C.V. based countries – all these C.V. suggestions can be used to great effect. For resume based countries – these suggestions work just as well for you. Let us start with the structure of your C.V. Note I say structure and not template. When you routinely check hundreds of C.V.'s as part of your job, you can spot the templates given out by job centres and Microsoft and they become boring and reflect a lack of individuality, confidence and ability to write – all factors you do not want to display in your C.V.

There are basically four different C.V. structures:

- **Chronological:** Which is the most common.
- **Functional:** Which is used for more "difficult" C.V.'s or when your experience far outweighs the expected qualifications?
- **Graduate:** Which is used by graduates seeking their first role, and who have little job experience.
- **Professional:** Which is used in academia, medical field etc. where multiple qualifications and published works are expected.

The following is the basic structure of the respective C.V.'s.

Chronological C.V.

This is the most common used and the one most often requested and expected by employers.

Table 1: Chronological C.V. Template

Name and Contact Details
Career Overview
Sometimes called personal statement
Qualifications
Latest first
Include professional qualifications
Technical and/or Computing Qualifications
Packages
This section is large for IT roles
Career Experience
Latest first

Functional C.V.

This is used when you are heavy on experience and achievements but short on the appropriate qualifications normally expected for this role. People returning to work after a long break can or those who have done a considerable number of jobs find this format helpful.

Table 2: Functional C.V. Template

Name and Contact Details
Career Objective
Key Achievements *Look for at least 3*
Key Skills *If you have a number use tables or bullets*
Qualifications
Career Experience *Overview only*

Student C.V.

This is best used by those newly out of college, university and school. It can also be used for those seeking second jobs.

Table 3: Student C.V. Template

Name and Contact Details
Career Objective *Include overview of your skills* *Include some key achievements*
Qualifications *Latest first* *Include professional qualifications*
Relevant Experience
Personal Achievements

Professional C.V.

This is used when the role expects that you have been published and passed a considerable number of extra qualifications. You use a Chronological C.V. and then list your qualifications in the usual area. Your publications are then listed at the end of the Career Experience.

Headers and Footers

When you send your C.V. off to an agency and they forward it to a potential employer, they always remove your contact details and sometimes your name as well. This means that the design of your C.V. can be unbalanced.

The way to avoid this is to include your contact details and name in the header and footer of your C.V. In this way, they can easily replace them with their own contact details without spoiling the balance of your C.V.

If you do not use agencies and send your C.V. off directly to a company, when your C.V. is printed off – your name and contact details are still there to be seen. In case your C.V. is only viewed on the computer – save it in print format and ensure that your name and contact details, including the phone number, are included on your email.

Your Name and Contact Details

You should provide your full name, address, email address and phone number upon which you can easily be contacted. This means a phone with voicemail attached. Do not include marital status, religion, number of children etc. It is not required. Age, ethnicity, disability etc is illegal in many countries – so do not include it. If you are a foreigner, confirm your work status or state if you need a work permit.

You should not use your company email address. Not only are they now regularly monitored, but also you are using your company's resources. Would you employ someone who looks for work in company time and steals company resources to do so? Thought not.

Career Overview or Personal Statement

Include your most important skills. What are the most important skills needed for the job you want? Consider including one or more of these as being required in the job that you seek. The implication here is that if you are looking for a job that requires 'Skills on a particular computer package,' then you have those skills. Of course, your interview and C.V. should support those skills with specific examples.

You should refer to the job advert for areas that they are particularly looking for. Be careful that your C.V. does not totally mimic the advert and reads naturally.

Ensure that your C.V. does not read like a string of clichés. You will be surprised how many C.V.'s I have seen from "organised, proactive individuals" etc. It is a bit like beauty contestants always wanting to work with children and animals!

Include specifics if these are important to you.

If you have substantial experience in a particular industry (such as 'Computer Controlled Machine Tools') or have a narrow and specific objective that you really want (such as 'Art Therapist with the Mentally Handicapped'), then it is OK to state this. But, in so doing, realize that by narrowing your alternatives down you will often not be considered for other jobs for which you might qualify. Still, if that is what you want, it just may be worth pursuing (though I would still encourage you to have a second, more general objective just in case).

Qualifications

Different levels of jobs require different jobs. If you have a degree then always state what kind of degree and the level you obtained. You should also state from what university or college you received your qualifications.

You should also include your high school qualifications, unless you have reached a more senior position where it does not matter any more. Many jobs require Maths and English qualifications and you should state you have these if you do.

If you have professional qualifications, these should also be listed. Date any qualifications gained as well as any appropriate level.

If you are at research and professor level, your books and publications should be noted at the end of your C.V.

Technical Skills

If you are seeking a non-IT role, you should include all your technical skills in a list. Please do not include such things as "internet" unless it is very relevant. If you use MsOffice, note this – not each individual programme, if only MsWord then this should be noted as such.

This is also a good area to note any languages you speak, with an idea of the depth of your skills.

Note any technical courses passed relevant to the position you are seeking at the top of this section, in reverse order of gaining them.

If you are seeking an IT role then this section is more important. You should note all computer languages, methods, packages, software, hardware and comms experience that you have. Include version and model numbers if relevant. Be very truthful – you will be tested by experts. I have lost count of the number of people who claimed to have skills they did not and could not answer simple questions about them at the interview. That is a quick "good bye"!

Career Experience

Here is where you list your career, latest role first. Use present tense for all current roles and past tense for past roles.

This is not the place to copy down your job description. Give a brief overview and then bullet your key responsibilities. Make sure they are yours and not just the team you worked with. Do not include excessive detail or ramble on.

There should be more information in the recent roles and much less in the far distant ones – unless they hold very important information.

You should not put your salary details or the reasons for leaving. There should be no unexplainable gaps.

Key Achievements

It is always good to have something on your C.V. to ensure that the reviewer remembers you. Your achievements are a good place to put this. Try for at least three- all business based if possible and all demonstrating some of the things the employer is seeking.

Key Skills

Make these appropriate to the job. If you are a career returner then identify some things you have done that demonstrate these business based skills. You should look at what the advert is asking for and include organisation, team leading, keyboard skills, administration, project leading etc. if appropriate.

Relevant Experience

Here is where you list your relevant experience, in reverse date order. Give depth of experience and length of experience as appropriate.

Personal Achievements

If you are a student or have little work experience then it is quite ok to use personal achievements instead. Make them large and relevant. Truthful of course – you never know when you might meet another champion bob sleigher who knows you are not speaking the truth!

Design of Your C.V.

You will not believe the appalling C.V.'s I have seen. Pink paper, odd shaped paper, multiple fonts, pictures and silly comments are not necessary.

Use good quality white A4 paper or MsWord if emailed. Keep colours to the minimum and your fonts to just one. Do not include your picture unless it is requested.

The only exception to this is for an artistic role – here you can be a bit more imaginative – but not silly. A hard worked reviewer soon gets tired of things that give them extra work or are silly.

Cover Letter

To be effective, your cover letter should follow the basic format of a typical business letter and should address four general issues:

Top of the Letter: Job reference.
First Paragraph: Why you are writing.
Middle Paragraphs: What you have to offer.
Concluding Paragraph: A polite closure.

At the top of the letter – using the word Reference: should be the references supplied in the advert as well as the title and if necessary, the level of the job for which you are you are applying.

You should also mention the publication or job site you where you saw the advert. Not only does this show you professionalism and care for details but it also helps the reviewer.

Anything that helps the reviewer gets your C.V. further up the "yes" pile as opposed to being on the "too much trouble pile"!

If a name if given on the advert apply to that name, if not Dear Sir/Madam is quite appropriate.

In some cases, you may have been referred to a potential employer by a friend or acquaintance. Be sure to mention this mutual contact, by name, up front since it is likely to encourage your reader to keep reading!

Also, at it does need mentioning, remember to put your name and address as well as a contact telephone number and email address – all of which should be private as opposed to company details.

In the first paragraph, you should state why you are applying. It could be something like..."This role particularly appealed to me because..." or "I am seeking a challenging role in the xxxx sector and I believe that I can contribute to your company by zzzz..."

More importantly, express your enthusiasm and the likely match between your credentials and the position's qualifications.

In the middle paragraph, you should identify a few of your achievements, qualifications, experience or abilities that make you particular appropriate for this role.

You should ensure that you are reasonably short and pithy, but also memorable. Do not fall back on those tired old comments about being a pro-active team member for example. This does little to advance your cause! Far more interesting is to hear about you saving a company £1,000's in your latest venture or your potholing in Peru for charity. Well you get the idea.

In the last paragraph, you should mention that you have enclosed/attached your current C.V., which you are happy to expand up or discuss if required. End with how much you are looking forward to hearing from them very soon.

Cover Letter Tips

Our first tip in writing a winning cover letter is to match your qualifications and education with those that the job is requesting. This is important because it shows that you are choosy with whom you apply to work with as well as showing a level of skill and care that will be particularly attractive to a future employer.

Take the job posting and make a list of the criteria the employer is looking for. Then list the skills and experience you have. Either address to how your skills match the job in paragraph form or list the criteria and your qualifications.

Then identify the key requirements and address them in your cover letter. Of course, your C.V. is the ideal place to highlight the other requirements.

Second tip is not to design a form letter and send it to every potential employer – this is quickly spotted and dealt with like any other on spec spam they get!

Our third tip is to emphasise your achievements and problem-solving skills. Show how your education and work skills are transferable, and thus relevant, to the position for which you are applying. If you are a seeking a senior role then emphasise your business achievements and what you have bought to recent companies you have worked for.

Lastly make your cover letter short, to the point, memorable and signed!

C.V. Check List

- Have you included everything including your name?
- Is it clear, concise, easy to read with no grammar or spelling mistakes?
- Does it answer the requirements of the job applications?
- Is it correct and does it accurately reflect your skills and experience?
- Has a good friend checked it through?
- Is it at least two pages and no more than three pages?

Tips On Writing Your C.V.

We've now understood the contents of the interview winning C.V. – so how do we go about actually writing it?

Grammar and spelling: NEVER over look spelling errors or typos. That is a one-way trip to the discarded file. Check and recheck. Typos and spelling errors usually occur when you try to do something at the last minute. So leave enough time to check it through and use a spell checker.

Tailor the objective to a given position or leave it out altogether. Objectives are helpful when you are trying to show the relationship between your skills and a particular position, but they merely annoy when they say inane things like "a challenging position suited to my education and skills." What position? What skills? C.V. readers will give yours, on average, seven seconds; do not make them cranky with filler.

Do not be vague. Be sure to customize your C.V. for each employer. The inability to do this, in some circumstances, e.g. when posting a C.V. on a job site, accounts for some of the low return rate on these applications. Anytime you try to do a "one size fits all" approach (by agency, computer, or just passing a C.V. around an organisation courtesy of a friend) you lose the all-important opportunity to craft the C.V. to fit a particular position.

Package your experience and skills correctly.

C.V.'s are read by people with little time that have a list of skills and experience they are looking for. If the job you are applying for calls for a marketing person with three years experience in the retail industry - then make sure that is how you present yourself.

What can you do for your future employer?

Employers employ new staff for specific reasons:

- They want to increase profits.
- They want to enter new markets.
- They want a particular role covered.
- They want to buy in new skills.

Make sure that your C.V. indicates what YOU can do for your new company. At this stage, you are a product for sale.

Do not be long-winded. Be pithy and keep it to one (preferably) or two pages unless you want a job in academia, research or the arts. IT contractors usually require that extra page as they, by definition, have more projects to describe.

Use verb phrases. -- "conceived campaign for student elections", "created online student newspaper", "and initiated weekly meetings for minority students "," lead charity drive" -- not sentences; this is not an essay or an obituary you are writing.

Use dates to show when you did things. Do not put just the vague "one year".

Students and Recent Graduates.

- Put your education up top and include relevant courses.
- Find out which skills the employer is seeking and be sure to showcase them.
- If you are short on actual job experience, include a HIGHLIGHTS or SKILLS SUMMARY section to "editorialize" about yourself a little.
- Be clear about what you want.
- If you intend to be both a full time student and a full-time employee, for instance, this might be a turnoff for some employers.

For New Graduates.

By definition, you will not have much work experience. Have an "experience" section because you can include internships, class projects and independent study to demonstrate your skills.

Sales Staff

For sales roles, you should include any targets you met as well as exceeded. Your C.V. should reflect your target based environment as well as the kind of things you can sell and through which media.

IT Staff

Your C.V. could be longer- say 3 pages, because you have more technical details to include. As agencies and employers always look for particular skills and experience, you should assist the reviewer by listing the major ones in your Technical area as well as within your experience area.

Senior Manager

At your level, your employer will want to know the size of teams and budgets that you have been your responsibility. Make sure to include these as well as giving a good idea of the level that you work at. Your C.V. should also be more achievement based as your employer will want you to make a significant difference to their company.

Professors, Medical etc

Your potential employer will want you to have published papers and books. List these at the end of your C.V. You may also need a 3 – 4 page C.V.

Company Application Forms

Fill out company applications completely - even if you have a C.V. Many companies require a completed application. Your willingness to complete one, and your thoroughness in doing so, will convey a great deal about your professionalism and abilities.

A Lesson in Bad C.V. Writing

I received this unrequested C.V. at my company – it was so awful it had to be included in this book. I print it here so that you can see if you can list the errors. After the C.V. I will give you the answers.

The first, of course, is that it was sent unsolicited to a company that does not employ these kind of staff. Also, it came attached to a blank email – so had to be fished out of the spam folder. Never, ever do this of course!

I have changed the name and contact details to protect the guilty. I have also sized it to fit this book – it was over A4 size to start with.

COVER LETTER

Dear Sir/ Madam,

As indicated in the enclosed resume, I have educationally earned a Bachelors degree in Advertising and Public Relations. I am fluent in English and Arabic with very basic information in the French language.

At present, I am seeking a position that will fully utilize my academic background combined with my skills and the experience I will gain from being a team member of your organisation, to advance in my career and develop your business

Thank you for your time and consideration.

Sincerely,

Mohamed El Saffilodom

Email: xxx@hotmail.com

Tel.: 099-12345678

Mohamed Osama EL Shafildom

International City, Spain Cluster, Bldg xxx, Apt G099

Mobile: 099-12345678

Email: xxxi@hotmail.com

<u>O</u>bjective	Seeking a challenging position in the field where my qualifications and skills may be developed and built upon in a developing career path.
<u>E</u>ducation	**Manor House School (M.H.S)** Thanaweya Amma, July 2000, **Modern Science and Art (MSA) with Middlesex University** Bachelor of Mass Communication, 2006-2007, Major: Advertising and Public Relations
<u>A</u>cademic Activities	**Head of Public Relations Committee, President of the Students Union [2004-2006].** • Organizing a training program for

	committee heads and 250 members.
	• Successfully planned and organised a "Talent Show", "Annual Show" and a "Talk Show", getting sponsors for the venue and refreshments.
	• Coordinated with the workshops to support trainings.
	• Directed the making of complete database of all participants and members.
	• Helped in security measures.
Work experience	**Barclays Bank (Egypt)** **SME's (Small & Medium Enterprises)** **Relationship Officer:** Contacting new customers . Offering the bank products to the customers . Opening accounts to companies (specially small & medium enterprises) . Remaining relationship with customer after opening the account . Solve problems that faces the customer . Offering the possibility of taking financial facilities . Getting new contacts from the customer to open accounts for them . **Coldwell Banker U.A.E**

Sales & Marketing Executive, Dubai, UAE.

- Discuss Customer's needs and goals in order to plan the search to find him the appropriate property.
- Provide preliminary estimate closing costs and down payment or rent requirement anticipated in the transaction.
- Discuss the positive and negative features of a property that may affect its value and future resale.
- Preview targeted properties in a timely way.
- Close the deal.

MSA University

Marketing Executive (Training), Cairo, Egypt. Summer 2006

- Communicate a clear message to parents and students who are applying for MSA University.

- Assisting in developing the marketing campaign including TV, radio, and newspaper ads.

ALAMIA Publishing & Advertising

Co.

Marketing Executive, Cairo, Egypt. 2005- 2006

- Organize Concerts and sports events (Auto Cross)
- Targeting Sponsors.
- Selling advertising spaces.

Courses

- Corporate banking SME's program

Skills	**Language Skills:** Fluent in spoken and written Arabic and English. Very basic knowledge of French. **Computer Skills:** Significant knowledge of MS-rd, Excel, PowerPoint and Internet.
Personal Information	**Marital status**: Single **Military Status**: Exempted **Nationality**: Egyptian **Date of Birth**: 26/01/1983.

Where do I begin - It looks awful!

Cover Letter:

- The contact details uses frames which were very difficult to copy to this book. Reviewers may want to print the details off, which is difficult if your computer and printer are not exactly the same as the writer. Also agencies use OCR software to read relevant parts of the C.V. They do not work with frames.
- The frame was a different size to the rest of the letter.
- The title Cover Letter is superfluous and not centred.
- The grammar is very poor.
- Spacing is not correct so that the sentence does not start at the edge.
- There is no space between the paragraphs.
- They have used sir/madam instead of my name – which they could have easily found out. A step up from "dear sir" – when I am a female!
- He did not say what kind of role he wanted at what level.
- He gave me linguistic skills and then proved he had awful English and gave me no job related skills.
- His "seeking a position..." statement says what he wants from a job but gave me absolutely no reason as to why I would want to employ him.

C.V.:

- He does not have his name and contact details on each page of the C.V.
- Again, it uses frames.
- It uses multiple fonts – including mixed fonts in the same sentence and some quite appalling fonts.
- He uses different colours, including the borders.
- He uses an underline in a really strange way.
- He tells me his marital status and military status – why?
- He tells me about his school but not what he did there.
- He does not tell me his Degree level and appeared to have earned a degree in 1 year as opposed to the usual 3 – 4 years.
- The spelling and grammar is poor.
- He uses part bullets and non-bullets.
- He has line spaces in strange places.

Please do not do any of these things with your C.V.

It will not surprise you that I wrote back and offered my services, but not an interview!

Weaknesses On Your C.V.

D o you have a unique circumstance that might raise a recruiter's eyebrows when reviewing your C.V.? Your first impulse might be just to lie about your past experience, but there are other ways still make yourself attractive to an employer without necessarily being deceitful.

Gaps in Work History

Many people have gaps in their work history. If you have a legitimate reason for major gaps, such as going to school or having a child, you can simply state this on your C.V. You could, in some situations, handle one of these gaps by putting the alternative activity on the C.V., with dates, just as you would handle any other job.

Minor gaps such as being out of work for several months; do not need an explanation at all. You can often simply exclude any mention of months on your C.V. Instead, just refer to the years you were employed such as "1993 to 1994" and any gap of several months is not apparent at all.

Being Out of Work

Some of the most accomplished people I know have been out of work at one time or another and one out of five people in the workforce experience some unemployment each year.

It is not a sin and many people who are bosses have experienced it themselves. However, the tradition is to try to hide this on the C.V.

One technique is to put something like "19xx to Present" on your C.V. when referring to your most recent job. This approach makes it look like you are still employed. While this might be an acceptable approach in some cases, it may also require you to have to explain yourself early on in an interview. This soft deception can start you off on a negative note and may not end up helping you at all.

If you are currently out of work, your other alternatives are to write the actual month that you left your last job or to write in some interim activity such as being self-employed. Even if that means that you are working at a temporary agency or doing odd jobs, it may be better than being deceitful.

Remember that many employers have experienced being out of work themselves and may have more understanding of your situation than you realize.

Changing Careers

This is a situation related to the one described above and would be handled with a skills C.V. A change in careers does require some justification on your part, so that it makes sense to an employer.

This should mean that you should present experiences where you have demonstrated ability in or preparation for success in a different occupational area.

Negatives in your Work History

There is no reason for a C.V. to include any details related to why you have left previous jobs -- unless, of course, they were positive. For example, leaving to accept a more responsible job is to your credit. If you have been fired, analyze why. In most cases, it is for reasons that do not have to do with your performance.

Most often, people are fired as a result of interpersonal conflicts. These are quite common and do not indicate that you will necessarily have the same problem in a different situation. If your performance was the reason, you may have to explain why that would not be the case in a new job.

The C.V. itself should present what you did well in previous situations. Leave the discussion of problems for the interview, and take time in advance to practice what you will say if asked.

Unrelated Job History

If your previous work experience is in jobs that do not relate to what you want to do next, your best bet is to use a skills C.V. The advantage of the skills C.V. in this situation is that it allows you to emphasise those transferable skills that you have developed and used in other settings.

Recent Graduate

If you have recently graduated, you probably are competing against those with similar levels of education and more work experience. If you do not have a lot of work experience related to the job you want, you will obviously want to emphasise your recent education or training. This might include specific mention of courses you took and other activities that most directly relate to the job you now seek. New graduates need to look at their schoolwork as the equivalent of work. Indeed, it is work in that it required self-discipline, completion of a variety of tasks, and other activities that are similar to those required in many jobs.

You also may have learned a variety of things that are directly related to doing the job you want and you should present these in a skills C.V. in the same way you might present work experiences in a chronological C.V.

You should also play up the fact, if you can, that you are familiar with the latest trends and techniques in your field and can apply these skills right away to the new job. In addition, since you are experienced in studying and learning new things, you will be better able to learn the new job very quickly.

A skills C.V. will also allow you to effectively present skills you used in other jobs (such as waiting on tables) even though they do not seem to relate directly to the job you now want. These jobs were also work experiences and can provide a wealth of adaptive and transferable skills that you can use, with some thought, to support your résumé's job objective.

Too Little Experience

Young people, including recent graduates, often have difficulty in getting the jobs they want since employers will often hire someone with more experience. In this case, you may want to emphasise your adaptive skills that would tend to overcome a lack of experience.

Once again, a skills C.V. would allow you to present yourself in the best light. For example, emphasizing skills such as "hardworking" and "learn new things quickly" may impress an employer enough to consider you over more experienced workers.

You should also consider expressing a willingness to accept difficult or less desirable conditions as one way to break into a field and gain experience. For example, "willing to work weekends and evenings" or "able to travel or relocate" may open up some possibilities that might appeal to an employer.

You should also look for anything that might be acceptable as experience and emphasise it. This might include volunteer work, family responsibilities, education, training, military experience, or anything else that you might present as legitimate activities that support your ability to do the work that you feel you can do.

Over Qualified

After a period of unemployment, most people become more willing to settle for less than they had hoped for at the beginning. If you are willing to accept jobs where you may be defined as overqualified, consider not including some of your educational or work-related credentials on your C.V. Moreover, be prepared to explain, in the interview, why you do want this particular job and how your wealth of experience is a positive and not a negative.

Not Sure of Job Objective

As I have mentioned on several occasions, including a job objective on your C.V. is highly desirable but not required. If you really cannot settle on a long-term job objective, consider on settling on a short-term one, and use that on your C.V. In some cases, you can also do several C.V.'s, each with its own job objective. This can make sense in some situations and will allow you to select information that will support your various options to best effect.

Less Education than Normally Required

If you have the previous experience and skills to do a job that is often filled by someone with more education, you should take special care in preparing the education and experience sections of your C.V.

For those with substantial work experience, you can simply not include a section on education at all. While this does have the advantage of not presenting your lack of formal credentials in an obvious way, a better approach might be to present the education and training that you do have without indicating that you do or do not have a degree.

For example, mention that you attended such and such a college or program but do not mention that you did not complete it. This approach avoids your being screened out unnecessarily and provides you with a chance at an interview that you might not otherwise get.

Major C.V. Writing Errors

C V's are a necessity for almost every job on the planet -- accountant, teacher, CEO or government employee. However, unless you carefully and objectively examine your C.V. before sending it out, recycling bins across the UK may be filling up with those ill-planned documents. Before mailing your next C.V., check the ten C.V. "do nots" below:

Structure Of Your C.V.

Not Considering how your C.V. will be Reviewed.

Many C.V.'s are now submitted via job sites on the internet or via agencies. Successful sites and agencies – and these are the ones you want working for you - use some kind of technology to review and store your C.V. This means that your C.V. must have two properties:

- Be able to be scanned – this means no columns, frames or tables, lined bullets only and a minimal amount of italics.

- The key words and describing information that the agency is looking for must be readily available on your C.V. For example, if they are looking for 3 year's financial experience, then this must be *easily seen* on your C.V. Do not expect your reviewer to take the time to work it out. This particularly applies to IT based C.V.'s, where all you technical skills must be available.

Does Size Matter?

If your career warrants a three-page C.V., then go ahead and create a document that reflects the full range of your experience and accomplishments. Do not reduce the type size to such a degree that your C.V. becomes difficult to read. Do not waffle on; thinking that the more you write the better you look!

No Extra Papers, Please

When you send out your C.V., do not include copies of transcripts, letters of recommendation or awards, unless you are specifically asked to do so.

If you are called in for an interview, you may bring these extra materials along in your briefcase for show-and-tell.

State Your Case

If you are seeking a job in a field in which you have no prior experience, do not use the chronological format for your C.V. By using a functional or skills-oriented format, you can present your relevant experience and skills up front.

Target Your Audience

Do not mail out your C.V. to every ad in the Sunday newspaper. If you are not even remotely qualified for a position, do not apply. Read the ads, determine if you have the right credentials and save the wear and tear on your computer and your nerves.

Design

Appearances Count

Do not try to save money by printing your C.V. on cheap copy paper instead of good quality stock. Check for typos, grammatical errors and coffee stains. Use the spellchecker feature on your word processor and ask a friend to review the C.V. to find mistakes you might have missed.

Too Short or Too Long.

Too many people try to squeeze their experiences onto one page, because they have heard that a C.V. should never be longer than one page. When formatting the C.V. to fit on one page, many job seekers delete their impressive achievements. The reverse is also true. Take the candidate who rambles on and on for pages about irrelevant or redundant experiences -- the reader will easily be bored. When writing your C.V., ask yourself, "Will this statement help me land an interview?" Only include information that elicits the answer "yes" to that question.

The rule about the appropriate length of a C.V. is that there is no rule. Factors that go into the decision regarding length include occupation, industry, years of experience, scope of accomplishments and education. The most important guideline is that every word in the C.V. should sell the candidate.

Using a Functional C.V.

When There Is a Good Career History.

One of the pet peeves cited by hiring managers is a candidate who describes his or her skills and achievements but does not connect them with a particular job. It is irksome not to see the career progression and the impact made at each position. Unless you have a C.V. emergency situation, such as virtually no work history or excessive job-hopping, avoid the functional C.V. format. One of the most effective C.V. formats is the modified chronological type. Here is the basic layout:

- Header (name, address, email address, phone number)
- Lead with a strong profile section (detailing the scope of your experience and areas of proficiency)
- Reverse chronological employment history (emphasizing achievements in the past 10-15 years)
- Education (this might be moved to the top for new grads)
- Other related topics include professional affiliations, community activities, technical expertise, publications/patents and languages spoken.

Not Including a Summary

or Profile Section That Makes an Initial Hard Sell.

A summary section is one of the greatest tools that a job seeker has. Candidates who have done their homework will know the type of skills and competencies that are important in the position. The summary should demonstrate the skill level and experiences directly related to the position being sought. To create a high-impact summary statement, peruse job openings to determine what features are important to employers. Next, write a list of your matching skills, experience and education. These selling points can then be incorporated into the summary.

References Available...

Employers know that if you are searching for a job, you should have professional references. Therefore, this statement mainly wastes space. Use it only as a graphical element -- to signal the end of a long C.V. or to round out the page design.

Use of Personal Pronouns

("I" and "me") and Articles ("an" and "the").

A C.V. is a form of business communication, which should be concise and written in a telegraphic style. There should not be any mention of "I" or "me" and only minimal use of articles. Here is an example:

The statement: I developed a new product that added $2 million in sales and increased the gross margin of the market segment by 12%.

Should be changed to: Developed new product that added $2 million in sales and increased gross margin of market segment by 12%.

Typos!

One typo can land your C.V. in the garbage. Two typos or more, and your chances are greatly diminished. Proofread, proofread, proofread, and show your C.V. to several friends to have them proofread it as well. This document is a reflection of you and should be perfect.

Contents

Truth or Consequences.

Do not fudge over dates or titles on your C.V. to hide the fact that you have been unemployed, that you switched jobs too frequently or that you held low-level positions. If a prospective employer conducts a background check and discovers that you lied, you can kiss the job good-bye.

Too Focused on Job Duties

One of the most prevalent C.V. blunders is to turn a C.V. into a boring listing of job duties and responsibilities. Many people even use their company job descriptions as a guide to developing their C.V.'s.

To create a C.V. that is a cut above the rest, you should go beyond showing what was required of you, and demonstrate how you made a difference at each company. Provide specific examples of how the company benefited from your performance. When developing your achievements, ask yourself the following questions:

- How did you perform the job better than others would have?
- What were the problems or challenges that you or the organisation faced? What did you do to overcome the problems? What were the results of your efforts? How did the company benefit from your performance?
- Did you receive any awards, special recognition or promotions as a result of your performance?

What Have You Done Lately?

While it is certainly acceptable to have a two-page C.V., do not list every single job you have ever held. Personnel managers are most interested in your experience from the last 10 years, so focus on your most recent and most relevant career experience.

Put Your Best Foot Forward.

Do not simply copy the job description jargon from your company's HR manual. To show that you are more qualified than the competition for the positions you are seeking, you need to do more than simply list your job responsibilities.

Present specific accomplishments and achievements: percentages increased, accounts expanded, awards won, etc.

No Excuses.

Do not include the reasons you are no longer working at each job listed on your C.V. The phrases "Company sold," "Boss was an idiot" and "Left to make more money" have no place on your C.V.

Getting Personal.

Personal information does not belong on a C.V. in some countries, especially in the United States and the UK. It is not recommended to include information on your marital status, age, date of birth, religion, race, height, weight etc. There are some exceptions, however, such as some entertainment professionals.

Listing Personal or Irrelevant Information.

Many people include their hobbies and interests, such as reading, hiking, snowboarding, etc. These should only be included if they relate to the job objective. For example, if a candidate is applying for a position as a ski instructor, he or she should list cross-country skiing as a hobby.

If you have reached some level of achievement in your hobby or interest, this can be included in order to show that you are a high achiever. However, you should be careful that you do not give the impression that this success is at the expense of your job.

C.V. Blunders

Every day, someone writes something on their C.V. that they wish they hadn't. Sometimes they do not even know they have done it, but wonder why they never are offered an interview. To give you a brief break - here are just a few that we have come across.

Typos and Grammar Slips

- "Suspected to graduate early next year."
- "Disposed of $2.5 billion in assets."
- "Proven ability to track down and correct errors."
- "Accomplishments: Oversight of entire department."
- "Strengths: Ability to meet deadlines while maintaining composer."
- "I am a rabid typist."
- "Here are my qualifications for you to overlook."
- "Work History: Performed brain wave tests, 1879-1981."
- "After receiving advice from several different angels, I have decided to pursue a new line of work."
- "Accounting cleric."
- "As indicted, I have over five years of experience analyzing investments."
- "Am a perfectionist and rarely if ever forget details."

- "Accomplishments: Completed 11 years of high school."
- "Fired because I fought for lower pay."
- "Size of employer: Very tall, probably over 6'5"."
- "Please disregard the enclosed C.V.—it is terribly out of date."
- "Finished 8th in my high school graduating class of 10."
- "Qualifications: No education or experience."
- "I am relatively intelligent, obedient and loyal as a puppy."
- "My compensation should be at least equal to my age."
- Reason for Leaving: My boss said the end of the world is near."
- "Reason for Leaving: The owner gave new meaning to the word 'paranoia.' I prefer to elaborate privately."

Bad Humour

What may seem funny to you soon gets very tiring and annoying to the poor person charged with reviewing hundreds of C.V.'s. Guess which ones are tossed to the discard pile? Here are a few of the bad humour C.V.'s I have heard of:

- "Title: Another C.V. from the 'Profiles in Excellence' series."

- "Note: Keep this C.V. on top of the stack. Use all others to heat your house."
- "Also Known As: Mr. Productivity, Mr. Clever or Mr. Fix-it."
- "Assisted in daily preparation of large quantities of consumable items in a fast-paced setting." (Translation: Short-order cook.)
- "But wait...there is more. You get all this business knowledge plus a grasp of marketing that is second nature."
- "I have an excellent track record, although I am not a horse."
- "My fortune cookie said, 'Your next interview will result in a job'—and I like your company in particular."
- "Trustworthy references available upon request— if I give them a few bucks."
- "Let's meet so you can 'ooh' and 'ahh' over my experience."

Sample C.V.'s

This is a fairly standard C.V. but they have highlighted their qualifications.

CHLOE ZABATSKI

123 Alpha Street • Las Vegas, NV 12345 • (123) 555-1234 • chloez@bamboo.com

---

OBJECTIVE: Position as Personal Assistant / Office Manager

HIGHLIGHTS OF QUALIFICATIONS

- 15+ years experience providing outstanding administrative and personal support to a senior executive.
- A motivated self-starter, able to quickly grasp issues and attend to details while maintaining a view of the big picture. Expert in juggling multiple projects and achieving on-time completion within budget.
- Creative, resourceful and flexible, able to adapt to changing priorities and maintain a positive attitude and strong work ethic.
- A clear and logical communicator, able to establish rapport with both clients and colleagues, and motivate individuals to achieve organizational objectives.

PROFESSIONAL EXPERIENCE

1988-pres. PERSONAL ASSISTANT & OFFICE MANAGER
Paige & Associates, Denver, CO

Personal Assistant

- Provided continuous, high quality support to President/CEO. Coordinated schedule, appointments and travel arrangements; managed expense account and recovery.
- Proofed and edited speeches, reports and press releases; screened calls and communicated directives to Board members and company shareholders.
- Managed President's securities portfolio and prepared regulatory filings as needed. Acted as liaison to stockbrokers, accountants and legal counsel.
- Organized annual shareholder meetings, including site selection, catering and preparation of appropriate materials.
- Planned two major relocations: Assisted in site selection, worked with architect on interior design, and oversaw equipment/furniture/telecommunications setup without interruption in operations.

Office Manager

- Coordinated work flow among five consultants and supervised three support staff. Prioritized and delegated tasks, provided motivation and direction to create a positive work environment and ensured accurate, on-time completion.
- Tracked office expenses and created monthly reports for senior executive. Prepared invoices, Accounts Receivable/Payable and banking.
- Mediated conflicts among employees and between staff and management, utilizing diplomacy and humor to resolve issues.
- Responded to client needs and provided additional support where necessary.

Additional experience includes:
Seminar and Retreat Coordinator, Meditation, Inc., Reno, NV
On-site Massage Therapist, Reno Corporate Massage, Reno, NV

EDUCATION & TRAINING

B.A., Psychology, American University, Washington, DC
CMT / Somatic Educator, Somatic Institute, New York, NY
Additional training includes: Stress Management and Meditation

---

This is a graduate C.V. with little relevant work experience so they have highlighted the content of their MBA.

RANDI B. JENKINS

134 Whaler Cove • Port Washington, NY 12345 • 123-555-1234 • rbjenkins@.bamboo.com

OBJECTIVE: Marketing or Marketing Management Position

HIGHLIGHTS OF QUALIFICATIONS

- May 2004 received M.B.A. Degree with emphasis in Marketing.
- Six years' experience in program development, international marketing, and Internet marketing.
- Highly effective leading and motivating teams to produce positive results while meeting deadlines.
- Strong communication, interpersonal, and presentation skills.

PROFESSIONAL MARKETING EXPERIENCE

COMTROTRON, New York, NY   2003 to 2004
Marketing Consultant / Graduate Student Intern

- Interned as marketing consultant for this international e-business development company.
- Became integral team member in the development of online marketing programs for clients including AT&T, Avon, and Nike.
- Developed reports for clients including Avon's "Customer Needs and Reports Strategy."
- Conducted extensive research on the Internet, analyzed information, identified online solutions, and reported results to project leaders and clients.

COOKING TIME INTERNATIONAL PUBLICATIONS, New York, NY   1998 to 2003
Publicity Manager

- Managed promotions and publicity campaigns for over 200 titles of international publishing company.
- Created promotional strategy, managed company website, and increased online promotions.
- Organized and conducted trade show presentations, promotional events, and seminars.
- On several occasions made guest appearances as a food expert for local network TV and radio stations.
- Made presentations on new directions and products at national and international cooking conferences.
- Supervised and trained staff of four including a publicist and marketing assistant.
- Pitched stories and secured placement in top 100 daily newspapers and high-profile magazines.
- Coordinated distribution of collateral such as catalogs, brochures, and point-of-sale materials.

LONDONMIST FRAGRANCES, London, England   1997 to 1998
Assistant to Publicity Director / Student Intern

- Assisted in coordination of promotional campaign that launched EveningMist line product, "Shades."
- Maintained departmental records and correspondence; coordinated and scheduled meetings.

EDUCATION AND TECHNICAL SKILLS

M.B.A., Marketing, New York University, New York, NY   2004

Relevant Coursework:	Brand Management	Marketing Strategy	Sales Channel Mgt.
Data Analysis	Sports & Events Mktg.	Global Management	Strategic Advantage
Leadership	Decision Modeling	Managerial Finance	Managerial Accounting

B.A., History, Adelphi College, Garden City, NY   1997

Technical Skills - Illustrator, Photoshop, Filmaker; MS Access, Excel, PowerPoint, QuarkXpress

This is a more conventional C.V. but from a career changer.

SARA FREMONT

5624 Oak Lane ~ St. Louis, Missouri 63031

314-555-1212   support@resumeedge.com

EDUCATOR
DRIVER & TRAFFIC SAFETY

Patient and caring Professional committed to helping students learn. Certified in driver and traffic safety from Midwest State University. Memberships include ADTSEA (American Driver Traffic Safety Education Association), MDTSEA (Midwest Driver Traffic Safety Education Association), and the National Association of Female Executives. Additional background as a Missouri Licensed Property Casualty Insurance Agent for Home, Auto, Health, and Life.

CERTIFICATION, LICENSURE, & EDUCATION

MIDWEST STATE UNIVERSITY, St. Louis, Missouri
Driver / Traffic Safety Education Certification, August 2002

~ Renewal of Missouri Educators License K-8, July 2002

MISSOURI EDUCATORS COLLEGE, St. Louis, Missouri
Graduate Level Coursework in Education, 1989-1990
G.P.A.: 3.83/4.00

Bachelor of Science Degree in Elementary Education, 1976
Semester Honors: 3.47/4.00   Semester Highest Honors: 4.00/4.00
Awarded compensated internship (for teaching)

PROFESSIONAL EXPERIENCE

FIRST CHOICE INSURANCE COMPANY, St. Louis, Missouri   April 1990 ~ July 2000
Insurance Agent
- Managed insurance agency daily operations, including territories and accounts.
- Fielded and resolved insurance sales questions; generated leads.
- Developed customer quotations and completed applications.
- Hired, trained, and motivated support personnel.
- Assessed client needs and established long-term client relationships.
Achievements:
  ➤ Acknowledged as line leader of a four state territory for loss ratio, retention, and customer service.
  ➤ Exceeded measured performance standards per ratios each of 10 years.

S&D RAILROAD COMPANY, St. Louis, Missouri   March 1979 – November 1987
Conductor
- Responsible for movement of freight traffic between pre-determined destinations.
Achievements
  ➤ The first female to be employed by this train service.
  ➤ Promoted from entry-level position within a very short period of time.

FRONTENAC SCHOOL DISTRICT, Frontenac, Missouri   October 1972 – March 1979
Transportation Department, Building & Grounds, and Substitute Teacher
- Employed during entire collegiate experience 20-40 hrs per week.

This is someone with the same employer but two different levels of job.

CHLOE ZABATSKI

123 Alpha Street • Las Vegas, NV 12345 • (123) 555-1234 • chloez@bamboo.com

OBJECTIVE: Position as Personal Assistant / Office Manager

HIGHLIGHTS OF QUALIFICATIONS

- 15+ years experience providing outstanding administrative and personal support to a senior executive.
- A motivated self-starter, able to quickly grasp issues and attend to details while maintaining a view of the big picture. Expert in juggling multiple projects and achieving on-time completion within budget.
- Creative, resourceful and flexible, able to adapt to changing priorities and maintain a positive attitude and strong work ethic.
- A clear and logical communicator, able to establish rapport with both clients and colleagues, and motivate individuals to achieve organizational objectives.

PROFESSIONAL EXPERIENCE

1988-pres. **PERSONAL ASSISTANT & OFFICE MANAGER**
Paige & Associates, Denver, CO

Personal Assistant
- Provided continuous, high quality support to President/CEO. Coordinated schedule, appointments and travel arrangements; managed expense account and recovery.
- Proofed and edited speeches, reports and press releases; screened calls and communicated directives to Board members and company shareholders.
- Managed President's securities portfolio and prepared regulatory filings as needed. Acted as liaison to stockbrokers, accountants and legal counsel.
- Organized annual shareholder meetings, including site selection, catering and preparation of appropriate materials.
- Planned two major relocations: Assisted in site selection, worked with architect on interior design, and oversaw equipment/furniture/telecommunications setup without interruption in operations.

Office Manager
- Coordinated work flow among five consultants and supervised three support staff. Prioritized and delegated tasks, provided motivation and direction to create a positive work environment and ensured accurate, on-time completion.
- Tracked office expenses and created monthly reports for senior executive. Prepared invoices, Accounts Receivable/Payable and banking.
- Mediated conflicts among employees and between staff and management, utilizing diplomacy and humor to resolve issues.
- Responded to client needs and provided additional support where necessary.

Additional experience includes:
Seminar and Retreat Coordinator, Meditation, Inc., Reno, NV
On-site Massage Therapist, Reno Corporate Massage, Reno, NV

EDUCATION & TRAINING

B.A., Psychology, American University, Washington, DC
CMT / Somatic Educator, Somatic Institute, New York, NY
Additional training includes: Stress Management and Meditation

---

This is a more artistic C.V. so the design is more striking!

SARA LIVINGSTON

1213 Flower ~ Beverly Hills, California 90210
800-555-1212 ~ support@resumeedge.com

OVERVIEW OF QUALIFICATIONS

- Award-winning, multi-lingual Interior Designer with an outstanding background in set design for NBC's *The Templetons*, TriStar's *Edge of Paradise*, and *Carrolton Returns* on PBS.
- High profile clientele includes Burt Williams, Trevor Sanders, Liz MacQuire, and R. Fredericks.
- Fluent in English, Spanish, Portuguese, German, and Italian; certified by the Design Institute of New York and Los Angeles; licensed designer in the United Kingdom, France, and Italy.

OUTSTANDING PROFESSIONAL ACCOMPLISHMENTS

- Chosen as *Designer of the Decade* in 1999 for work on *The Templetons* series.
- Received special Academy Award in 1992 for work on *Edge of Paradise*.
- Featured in *Vanity Fair, Time Magazine, Newsweek, Elle,* and *Interior Design.*
- Recognized as the youngest design entrepreneur with the launching of *Designs by Sara.*

EMPLOYMENT HISTORY

DESIGNS BY SARA, New York, Los Angeles, Rome, and London   1990 - 2001
Founder / President
- Established interior design / boutique catering to high net-worth clientele, including stars of stage, screen, and television.
- Oversaw daily operations, including purchasing, outsourcing, and client relations.
- Collaborated with online firm for *Designs by Sara* training course accredited by the Design Institute of New York and Los Angeles.
- Grew company from $5.5 million in 1990 to $6 million annually in 1993.
- Recruited, trained, and directed activities of 17 design professionals.
- Launched satellite offices in Los Angeles in 1992, Rome in 1993, and London in 1994.
- Wrote weekly column in the *Los Angeles Times Magazine* on affordable interior design.
- Appeared on local newscasts with design tips.

COVENTRY INTERIORS, New York, New York   1989 - 1990
Intern
- Participated in client / designer meetings.
- Created design for firm's reception area that was chosen as best among 20 interns.
- Assisted junior designers with fabric, furniture, and accessory selection.

ACADEMIC BACKGROUND

DESIGN INSTITUTE OF NEW YORK, New York, New York
- *Master of Arts in Interior Design, 1989*
- *Awarded the Francois Designation for Outstanding Interior Design Work, 1988-1989*

DESIGN INSTITUTE OF LOS ANGELES, Los Angeles, California
- *Bachelor of Arts in Interior Design, 1988*

ASSOCIATIONS

- *Vice-President*, Interior Designers of America, 1999-Present
- *Member*, European Designers, 1997-Present

Artistic and showing lists of exhibitions etc. and a more colourful background.

Dawn Toor

213.555.1212 ~ support@resumeedge.com

4431 Eastwick Village Drive ~ Charlotte, NC 11803

Artist

Award-winning Designer with degrees in Textiles and Oriental Painting. Background includes exhibiting work at the Manchester Gallery and successfully completing an internship with Ralston Technology in the United States. Fluent in English, Spanish, and Russian.

Awards & Exhibitions

> Third Place, LG Chemicals Design Contest, sponsored by LG Chemicals, Ltd., 1996
> Second Place, Textile Design Contest, sponsored by US Federation of Textile Industries, 1995
> Third Place, Noonan Design Contest, sponsored by the Noonan Company, 1995
> Third Place, US Modern Art Concours, 1994
> Five-time Recipient, Department Scholarship, 1992-1994

> Department of Textile Art Degree Exhibition, 1997
> Best Graduate Exhibition, Manchester Gallery, 1995
> Department of Oriental Painting Degree Exhibition, 1995
> Department of Oriental Painting Exhibition, 1994-1995
> US Modern Art Exhibition, 1994

Professional Experience

RALSTON TECHNOLOGY, INC., New York, USA   1999 – 2000
Intern, Art Department

- Successfully completed the presentation CD involving draping cars for Hyundai Motor Company of Korea.
- Concluded training for the Artworks Studio software GTxL cutter system.
- Traveled to Atlanta for the Bobbin Americas Expo from September 30 to October 2, 1999.

FIRST IMPORTS CHANNEL, CO., LTD., London, UK   1997 – 1998
Designer, Flooring Design Department

- Designed flooring products and conducted market research to determine client needs.
- Ensured quality of color matching by working closely with the manufacturer.

Education

WESTFALL UNIVERSITY, Bridgeport, Connecticut
Bachelor of Fine Arts, Department of Textile Art, 1997

NEW HAVEN COLLEGE, New Haven, Connecticut
Bachelor of Fine Arts, Department of Oriental Painting, 1995

A functional C.V. with a slightly different but very readable layout.

Tom Fitzgerald

6642 Overton Road
Portland, Oregon 97201
(503) 555-1212 ~ support@resumeedge.com

PROFILE
- Seasoned Professional with 20 years of experience in sales and sales management.
- Consistently awarded for outstanding performance; repeatedly won the *President's Club Award*, placing in the top 10% of company sales nationwide.
- Excels in public relations, marketing, human resources, and procedures administration.
- Licensed Real Estate Agent in the states of Oregon and California.
- Facilitates financial and business decisions for resort real estate companies.

EXPERIENCE

SALES MANAGEMENT
- Recruited, interviewed, hired, and trained all sales personnel.
- Managed all public relations, marketing, and sales for *Seasons Plus Resorts*, the largest vacation ownership company in the world.
- Developed an elite, goal-centered, cooperative sales force.
- Implemented and monitored productive property owner referral program.
- Directed site that was judged #1 within company in revenue per guest.

SALES
- Sold resort home sites as well as vacation properties to a marketed clientele.
- Won numerous awards as top performer and closer at all levels, including *President's Club Award* for sales in top 10% of the company nationwide.
- Directed building and sales of speculative property.
- Successfully completed sales leadership courses: "Dare to Soar" and "7 Habits of Highly Successful People."

ADMINISTRATION
- Grew company to $.5 million annual sales; broadened business scope from constructing small homes to developing high-end real estate properties.
- Bought property and oversaw home construction from start to finish.
- Hired all subcontractors and managed all payroll, insurance and taxes.

EMPLOYMENT

Director of Sales / Sales Manager, Seasons Plus Resorts, Portland, OR	2/99 – Present
Owner, Tom Fitzgerald Construction, Redding, California	6/90 – 12/98
Sales Professional, Seasons Plus Resorts, Portland, OR	6/85 – 5/90
Sales Professional, World Resorts, Portland, OR	4/82 – 5/85

EDUCATION

CIVIL ENGINEERING Western Tech, Portland, OR	9/76 – 5/78
BUSINESS California Community College, Redding, CA	9/75 – 5/76

Job Searching Strategies

Introduction

Finding a Job is hard work. So you think a job is work? It is nothing compared to the work that you will do while looking for one. In fact, career counsellors suggest turning your job hunt into an eight-hour-a-day, aggressive search in order to yield prime offers, or offers at all!

Moreover, since more companies are promoting from within, more mothers are returning to work and college graduates are getting more aggressive, the battle for jobs is tougher than ever before.

Steps In Your Job Campaign

Let us identify some of the steps you should take for a successful job search campaign.

The first step is you have to have a real desire for change. Which includes willing to put up with the stress and time and possibly expense of a job search and giving up some of what you have now if you will be leaving one job for another?

Secondly, you need to have to have a positive motivation. The sense that you are going to something new rather than running away from where you are is the won that will find your next career move.

Thirdly, it is very important to network. You want to speak to people in your new job, or profession, or company, to find out what are the skills, and the attributes, the characteristics, that would be necessary to succeed there. You also want to identify potential new employers and job leads.

When you have done that, you are in a good position to put together your C.V., a good modular cover letter and then to follow up with phone calls to those individuals you have contacted. We will help you at www.JobSuccess.co.uk and www.ResumeGuys.com

Not Sure What You Want To Do?

Many people say, "What if I want a life and not just a job? How do I balance these two?" In addition, there are really two things you have to remember.

First, that the degree of devotion you have to the mix between job and the other aspects of your life is up to you. If you are willing to give up on some career progress for the sake of family or other interests, that is fine. Just know the price you are willing to pay for what you want to gain.

The second thing to keep in mind is that there is an influence of your job on the rest of your life and there is an influence of the rest of your life on your job, so that you will never be able to separate the two completely.

How do you figure out what you want to do?

If you are thinking about your first real job or changing the kind work that you do, I suggest two steps.

First, there are a number of good vocational guidance tests that you can take at minimal expense. These would help you get some insight, identify your strengths and things you like or do not like.

The second step is just as important. Speak to people in various lines of work and various industries. Find out what they like about their work, how they do their job, what are some of things they would rather do without. Then compare what they tell you to your own preferences. This will help you identify a good type of job that you will find satisfying.

What personal characteristics will help/hurt my efforts to find a new job?

Three personal characteristics will help you in your job search effort.

First, be patient, it takes time to find your next good job.

Secondly, be persistent. You are going to find disappointments along the road, but if you keep on going you are going to find the job you want.

Third, remember always to be polite. Sometimes our frustration or concern comes out as anger or rudeness towards people we really want to think well of us.

Two characteristics can be very, very dangerous. One is feeling entitled, "Somebody owes me a job." "I work hard." "I did well." "I'm a smart person." That may all be true but nobody owes you anything. You have to earn everything you are going to get.

The opposite of that is feeling endangered. "If I do not have a job tomorrow I do not know what's going to happen." Well, what is going to happen is you are going to look for a job tomorrow and the next day and if you are a person with talent, you will get a good job.

Not Been Working For Some Time.

Some people have been out of the labour force for a number of years and they wonder how their job search might be the same or different from someone else. Some things are the same.

- You want a new job, and that is an important part of the process.
- Secondly, you are a talented person.
- Third, you are going to need to have to have a realistic attitude about the job search process and the world of work.

Some things are different.

- One is your work experience is not as current as other people who did not leave the work force for any period of time.
- Secondly, because you have been away from the work force, you are not as well connected in any professional network.

- Thirdly, your age and stage are no longer in tandem. That is, people your age who stayed in the labour force probably have overall, better positions, and more responsible positions where they have been working. If you can remember that you still have strengths, and talents you can contribute, but that getting back into the work force will be a little bit more difficult, you can and will be successful.

Your Career In A Changing Economy

Many people are concerned that the dramatic changes in the economy and the rapid pace that those changes are taking place mean it is not possible to have a career. It is really better for us to think that a career now means something different than it did for our parents or our grandparents. It is true that we are not going to start out on a certain path when we are 18 or 20 years old, stay on that path, and retire in 50 years.

We are going to have different jobs; we are going to have different employers. So now, we want to look at a career as something that gives us satisfaction over a long period, even if our title is different or if our profession is different. It may mean less job security, but it probably means more personal freedom.

Is there such a thing as employment security today?
Employment security today means more than doing a good job for your current employer. Because of downsizing, the job you have today may not be there tomorrow. Therefore, job security now means being an attractive employee for another employer if that need should arise.

Networking

I have heard a lot about networking. What is it? Many studies have shown that some jobs are filled, without being advertised, through a process called networking. What is networking? It means building contacts with people who can help you learn more about a job or industry and can also help you identify jobs when or even before they become open. As contacts lead to more contacts, you develop a network.

Is all this networking really necessary?

Some people have said to me, "You know, I just want a job. Is all this networking really necessary? Well, first, do you mean a job or the best possible job for you?

Secondly, since the majority of the jobs filled in the United States every year are through networking, it is a good idea to use this process even though it is a little less direct than you might be used to.

Whom Should I Try To Meet?

It is a good idea to think broadly about the people you would like to meet as you are building your network. Anybody who has a job similar to the job you want, works for a firm you are interested in, or is in the same industry could be helpful to you. However, why would they spend time talking to you?

One reason would be a sense of professional obligation - to help a colleague in the industry move on to their next step. By the way, someday you might be able to return the favour to them.

A second reason is social obligation. If you were somebody's relative, neighbour, or friend, people feel a sense of social obligation to help.

Some people say, "I do not know anybody in the field I want to enter. How can I start building a network?" One good way is to speak to family, friends, neighbours, the friends of neighbours, the neighbours of family members. These are people that have a kind disposition to you; they have a sense of social obligation.
If you extend from your family and from your friends and your neighbours, you will find at least one person who is doing the kind of job that you want.

A second source is professional associations. People in professional associations are usually very willing to help somebody who wants to join in their profession. You can get information about the professional associations in a good reference library.

A third thing you can do is read your local business news. If somebody's name is mentioned in the paper you might want to drop a note to them, reminding them what you read about in the paper and saying that you would like to discuss the issue in greater depth.

Network, network, network. Family, friends, leads through professional organisations, job directories and career fairs are the way 60% to 75% of job hunters finally land their prized positions.

You may not want to listen to it, but if your mother's cousin's accountant is looking for an assistant, you should follow the lead. The least you will do is develop more contacts and maybe even the job.

Do not, however, feel that it is always "who you know" that is going to land you a job. It may get you in the door, but no employer is going to hire you unless you are qualified.

Self Marketing

Although identifying the job you really want is a critical first step on its own, it is not enough to produce the desired outcome. Market research and a well-executed self-marketing campaign are needed to turn your goal into reality.

Once you have defined what you want, go out and talk to people who are doing what you want to do. Ask them how they got into the field, what path they travelled prior to landing their current position.

This process, often called information interviewing, is a valuable way to build your network of contacts inside organisations and your base of knowledge about fields and specific jobs you are pursuing. As part of the information gathering process, those considering career or industry changes, should visit their local libraries; there are great books today on a diverse range of careers.

Once you have taken stock of your interests and strengths, it is time to put together the marketing tools that can help you land the job you want. Your C.V. is the key marketing tool, your marketing brochure if you will.

A well-designed, error-free C.V. can go a long way to getting you into the select group of applicants who will be offered interviews. www.JobSuccess.co.uk or www.ResumeGuys.com will help you.

Ethical Issues

What ethical issues are involved In the job search process or in accepting offers? There are some important ethical issues for you to remember in a job search process.

- First, pursue jobs in which you have a reasonable and sincere interest.

- Secondly, make sure that everything you tell an employer is honest, whether it is on your C.V., in your cover letter, or at your interview.

- Third, if an offer is extended to you, and you say yes, make sure you are going to live up to that acceptance. In addition, you should notify other employers that you need to withdraw from the job search process.

Job Searching and Technology

A dvances in technology can provide you with some additional ways to look for a job. For example, traditionally you would send one C.V. to every employer of interest to you. That is fine, but now you can also send your C.V. to very reliable databases that employers access when they have a particular need and that way your C.V. is available to more employers and its available 24 hours a day.

Another great advantage for you is accessing information on your own computer, or on a computer in your reference library. Rather than running from book to book, you can now sit at a terminal and access information in a matter of minutes that used to take hours to collect.

The Internet can be a useful tool in your job search. Let us look at some ways. Most professions today have a web site on the Internet. It is a good place to find out who is involved with your profession. What are the current issues? What are people talking about?

Second, visit company web sites. You can learn a great deal about a company just by turning to their home page.

Third, the Internet has turned a good part of the world, into one big convention. You can do some long-distance networking just by using the Internet.

Technology can be a useful tool in your job search, but there are some things to be careful about. One is your own attitude. Remember there is no such thing as a magic bullet. Even with technology, finding a good job requires preparation and hard work.

Second, if you submit your C.V. to a database, it is possible that your own employer could access it. Before you submit that C.V., find out what safeguards you have. With all technology, remember, you can utilize a C.V. database but do not rely on it. There is no substitute for your own preparation and hard work. With a database, many employers will have access to your data.

It is a good idea to be prepared in case you hear from somebody unexpected. It is much better to say, "I'm very glad that you called," or "I'm very excited about meeting with you," than to say, "I just do not know what you're talking about," or "I haven't even heard of your company."

Should I send my C.V. off on Spec?

It is true that you can deliver your C.V. by e-mail quickly, but is it a good idea? Yes, if the employer has requested that you send your C.V. Otherwise, I recommend against it. Many employers get very annoyed when their e-mail accounts get cluttered with C.V.'s that they did not request.

You would have to be very lucky and send in your C.V. at the same time that they are looking for people just like you – otherwise you will go straight to the delete button!

Many job seekers with whom I've worked tell me of great frustration because they submit many copies of one generic C.V. to anyone receiving C.V.'s, without any customization or real understanding of the employer, and then wait in vain for replies. This strategy rarely works for anyone.

Unless you have specific technical skills for which you know an organisation is looking, based on your reading of journals and other professional sources in your field, do not waste your time applying for jobs this way. Blanketing the universe electronically without real contacts in organisations here is not likely to get you far!

Applying Online

Should you send your C.V. in an attachment? You are right and wrong at the same time. C.V.'s DO look better when they get sent as attachments, but increasingly employers are asking applicants *not* to send their C.V.'s as attachments because of the danger of viruses. Online job search experts are advising that some companies automatically delete all e-mail with attachments. Therefore, you may find that your beautiful C.V. never gets read.

Many job sites now have facilities to upload your C.V. Learn how to do this and use this method.

Your Web Personae And Your C.V.

If you put your web site on your C.V., ensure that there are only things on there that you want a potential employer to see. What may be cute and funny for your family and friends is not what an employer wants in their future branch manager!

The same thing happens with answering machines. When you apply for a job and list your number, forget the cute or funny message on your answering machine. Big mistake! If you want a Web page to be part of your portfolio for a job that requires Internet expertise, include it. However, please -- check it over for "audience appropriateness."

Just remember that it is very common to use search engines to find out about prospective employees. If you have entries on community sites such as MySpace and FaceBook – just make them ones that you want a future employer to see. If not use alias!

Job Fairs

Many people either do not know about job fairs or shy away believing they are not important enough to be chased or that the job fair will be so crowded that they will not get a look in! This is far from true. As the name states, the fairs are there with the one task of gaining potential employees so they are set up to attract the best in the easiest way. An extension of the job fair is the "Milk Round" which is a group of large companies visiting universities with the sole purpose of attracting the best soon to be graduates they can find.

The great advantage of visiting a job fair – providing it is one that is appropriate to the roles you are seeking – is that you get a chance to talk to people actually doing the job you are interested in as well as being able to compare a number of different companies in one day.

However, they are busy and if you are not prepared, you will not be able to make the best of their opportunities.

Here are some of the things that a job seeker must have by the time they are at the job fair in order to make the most out of it:

Advanced Research

The best place to find future job fairs is via appropriate internet searches as well as reading professional periodicals. Usually, the organisers of these events provide details of the contributing companies. Obtaining some information about the companies and the position that is open for the job would be an edge over the others.

Enough C.V.'s

Obviously, the most important thing to bring with them enough C.V.'s About 30 is a good number – even more if it is a large fair. You should keep your C.V.'s in a firm binder or folder so that they remain in good condition, not creased and without coffee stains! Many fairs also require you have to a collection of business cards as well. Many stands have competitions or give out magazines and books etc. in exchange for your business card. You can clip one to each C.V. as well. Do not forget to clip or staple your C.V. together as well as put your name and contact details on *each* page!

Approach Each Appropriate Stand

When you get to the fair, get hold of the show catalogue and plan out your day's work. The most popular stands will get very busy in the evenings and lunch time because this is when the local workers will call in!

When you have decided which stands to visit work your way around, stopping to talk to the relevant stand holder about their company and how you might fit into it. Be polite and interested – you will be remembered! The conversation will be two way as they will want to learn about you as well as know that you are interested in their company. This is also a good opportunity for new graduates and people looking for new careers to learn what the job involves. At the end of the conversation – which will be quite short – they will ask for your C.V. and place it in a box at the back of the stand. Many have different boxes for different jobs; some have boxes for people they are particularly interested in learning more about. So a chance to see how well you came across. It also explains why your CV should have your name on each page!

Dress For Success

As always, first impressions last. So dress as if you were going to an interview – which in fact you are. Dress comfortably with good solid shoes – job fairs are hard work and a sweaty, foot sore potential employee does not look good.

After the Fair

From the above description of the fair, you will understand that the exhibitors will have seen a lot of people and collected a lot of C.V.'s so do not be surprised if you do not hear anything for a few weeks. Of course, if you hear the next week that either means your C.V. went into the "very interested" box – or the company is efficient or did not receive many applicants.

It stands to reason that you should keep a list of all the companies that you gave your C.V. to for further information! You should refer to this when they contact you so that you appear to have researched them as opposed to sprinkling your C.V. around!

After a few weeks, it is quite permissible to drop an email or letter to confirm your continued interest.

Your Job Search Plan

Have a detailed plan of action and stick to it. There is no way anybody can stay organised without a written plan.

Planning carefully lets you predict where you are going, track your time, evaluate your progress and make sure productivity is maximized. Since the number of people you are in contact with could be in the hundreds, organisation is very important and almost vital. How else can you nurture each contact effectively? Information kept in a loose-leaf notebook or personal organiser reminds you of who you are supposed to contact on what date, names of further references, addresses and phone numbers.

Your job search plan should include:
- Ensure you have an effective C.V.
- Define your monthly and weekly goals.
- Find out information about companies that may need your skills.
- Identify job sites that deal with your type of job, job level, market and country.
- Identify newspapers and magazines that include adverts or company information in your target job search environment.

- Identify job agencies or job search agencies that may manage job vacancies you may be interested in – keep in regular contact with them.
- Find companies that are growing or hiring and research them.
- Target three new companies to contact per day.
- Visit your target job sites each day.
- Answer all relative adverts as soon as your target publications are available.

Interview Techniques

Interview Preparation

Ask anyone what their five most enjoyable ways of spending a working day would be and you can be pretty certain that attending an interview will not be one of them, even for the interviewer.

An interview is often seen as an inevitable ordeal, but it does not *have* to leave you with the feeling that you should just crawl back into the woodwork. It can be a good, perhaps even enjoyable experience and there are ways of increasing your chances of success.

You need to have a "master plan" and to develop ways of taking control of the interview. This does not mean fixing the interviewer with a menacing look and recounting your experience and qualities at breakneck speed. The way in which you take control needs to be balanced and well judged, that is, weighing up how much to say about what and how to present yourself.

Vital first impressions are important so make sure you are punctual and well groomed. Sit up straight in the chair, without folding your arms. Speak clearly and maintain constant eye-to-eye contact. Looking at the floor, walls or into the distance creates an image of wanting to be elsewhere.

Perhaps most important, try to be energetic and enthusiastic and sell yourself well. Acting cool and aloof tends to demonstrate arrogance, to which most employers will take an instant dislike. **Most of all 'prepare.'** Know the company that is interviewing you, know what they do and whom their competitors are and be prepared for them to ask such questions.

For years, experienced interviewers have been taught to use a variety of techniques. Now here is your chance to employ some of those same techniques yourself.

Think ahead: Spend a minimum of one hour and a maximum of an evening planning what you want to achieve. Too little time and you will not cover all the important issues; too much can be overkill.

Think about what impression you want to create: What important things in your past experience you want to talk about with you. What you are good at and not good at. Above all, think about things that you have done that mark you out from the crowd. Keep it genuine. A few embellishments may be acceptable, but outright lies are not.

Draw up a crib sheet: Research the company before the interview, read the papers or relevant professional journals and get hold of any in-house newsletters or promotional literature to get ideas for specific questions

Nine Steps To Perfect Preparation

There are nine important steps for you to take preparing for your job interview. Let us go over each one briefly.

First: Use your C.V. Have a friend ask you "how" or "why" about each line. This experience will help you get a better understanding of your own motivation, thought process and accomplishments. These three elements an employer will find important in an interview.

Second: Be able to articulate how the employer's needs are being met by your skills and experience.

Third: Be able to articulate your own motivation for being interested in that particular job. What attracts you to that particular company? In addition, what is your interest in that industry or profession?

Fourth: Be prepared for behavioural questions. Interviewers want to know what you did in actual situations or an example of certain behaviours that are important to the job.

Fifth: Practice answering some background questions that are commonly asked.

Sixth: Research the firm and its industry. Know the firm's major product or service. Have they been profitable? What challenges will they face over the next 3 to 5 years?

Seventh: Be sure to have at least five good questions ready to ask about the job, the firm, the industry or profession and external influences.

Eighth: Practice interviewing with a friend. Be sure to play the role of both the interviewer and the job applicant.

Ninth: Remember the interviewer is smarter and more experienced than you are – do not try to fool him or pretend you know something that you do not.

Frequently Asked Questions

There are many questions about interviews that get asked again and again so I've put together my own FAQ's.

What is a typical interview structure?

How many interviews should I expect with any one employer?

Although there is no set rule, a typical interview is scheduled for about one hour. In addition, there will be several phases in that interview. The first is should I expect an icebreaker, a few minutes of pleasant chitchat just so that you and the interviewer will feel comfortable with each other. Then the interviewer will get into some substantive questions, behavioural questions, questions about your background, and that will take 15, 20 to 25 minutes.

Usually the employer will leave 5 or 10 minutes for you to ask questions of the employer. That is a very important part of the interview and you should be well prepared.

Then there will be a close. The interviewer will thank you for coming in. In addition, you will have the opportunity to tell the interviewer what a pleasure it was to be there and how much you want the job. Usually, you will have to interview a second time, perhaps even a third time before getting a job offer.

What should I ask at an informational interview?

When you go to an informational interview, it is important that you bring some very good questions with you. For example:

- Can you tell me how your career has developed?
- What skills are necessary to be successful in this profession?
- What do you enjoy most about what you are doing?
- What do you enjoy least?

What am I really being asked at an interview?

What is it that the interviewer actually wants to hear? Some people wonder, "They're asking me all these questions at an interview, what can they learn about me from those questions and what is it, they really want to hear?" Three themes run through your interview.

- The first is, "Why should we hire you?"
- The second is your motivation, "Why do you want to work for us?"
- The third is did you come prepared, which translates to, "What do you know about our company? Or our profession?"
- Fourth is "Will you fit into our company?"
- Lastly, "What will we get out of hiring you?"

What the employer wants to hear is honest answers, giving good reasons why you should become their employee.

What if I am not sure that I want the job when I go to the interview?

It is very important to let the employer know and to be confidant that you really want the job. What if you are feeling, "I'm not sure I want this job, I need to know more about it??" Your job at the interview is to get the offer. Once you have the offer, you can make a decision whether you want to accept it or not. Therefore, I recommend two steps. Focus on those reasons that you want the job. Even if it were not the only job that you would ever consider. Remember, that you do not have to be certain about this particular job.

How important is proper dress to interview success?

The key point to remember about dress is that it is something you want to neutralize. That is, you are not going to gain points for wearing fancy or expensive clothes. You simply do not want to lose points for being improperly dressed. Dress professionally, modestly and conventionally.

What should I know about the company before the interview begins?

It is very important that you research the company before you go into the interview room. What kinds of things should you know? What is that firm's main product or service? Have they been profitable? Who are their competitors? How long have they been in that line of business? What are some of the challenges that they face over the next 3 - 5 years?

Where can you find information about companies? Well, it is readily available. For example, most public firms have an Annual report where they disclose the answers to all the things that we just mentioned, plus many more. You can use the library or the internet to get information about current events that affect that company or its industry.

What is the question-answer-question cycle?

The answer you give to any question may give the interviewer material for the next question. We refer to that as the question-answer-question cycle. Therefore, when you are preparing answers for a question, include some material that you would like the interviewer to follow up on. Examples are an extremely important part of your answer - they give your answer both context and credibility.

How long should my answers be?

How will I know if I have answered the interviewer's questions?

Your answers should be informative but concise. As a rule of thumb, think in terms of six or eight sentences.

If you are not sure if you have answered the question fully, feel free to ask. "Have I answered your question?" or "Would you like me to tell you more about that?" It is always a good idea to pause before you give your answer.

After all, an interview is a business meeting between equals. At business meetings, people pause and reflect before providing a response.

Say, "That's a good question. I need to think about that for a moment." Some people are worried that they are going to go blank at an interview.

Why do interviewers ask if I have any questions for them?

Employers usually give you time to ask questions of them. They have two reasons for doing this. One is simple courtesy; they have been asking you questions, so you should be able to ask them questions in return. A second reason is this: your questions are an important means of evaluating your fitness for the job. In fact, your questions could be as important as your answers.

What is the best way for me to close an interview?

At some point, the interviewer is going to thank you for coming in and wish you the best of luck. Some job candidates just say, "Thank you," and leave but that is a mistake. The proper way to close your interview is to say, "Thank you, I've enjoyed being here. I hope you are going to offer me this job. What's our next step?"

Is the interview over when it is over, or do I still have work to do?

After you leave the interview room, you might feel very relieved and think, "I'm glad that's over." Well, it is not really over yet. It is important to take notes about what happened. What was the first question? How did you answer it? How did the interviewer follow up on your answer? What was the second question, and so on?

What questions made me feel very confident? What questions made me feel uncomfortable? These notes will come in very handy if you are invited for a follow up interview with that company, if you interview for a similar job, or with a similar company. Moreover, you can also look over those notes and see what you can do to improve your interview techniques the next time.

It is also important and courteous to send thank you letters or emails to those people who spent time interviewing you that day.

If you gained the interview via an agent then you will, of course, review matters with them.

Interview Tips

The interviewing stage of your job search is the most critical. You can make or break your chance of being hired in the short amount of time it takes to be interviewed. Anyone can learn to interview well, since most mistakes can be anticipated and corrected. The following top 25 interviewing techniques will give you a winning edge.

Bring extra copies of your C.V. to the interview.

Nothing shows less preparation and readiness than being asked for another copy of your C.V. and not having one. Come prepared with extra copies of your C.V. You may be asked to interview with more than one person and it demonstrates professionalism and preparedness to anticipate needing extra copies.

Dress conservatively and professionally.

You can establish your uniqueness through other ways, but what you wear to an interview can make a tremendous difference. It is better to overdress than under dress. You can, however, wear the same clothes to see different people.

Be aware of your body language.

Be alert, energetic, and focused on the interviewer. Make eye contact. Non-verbally, this communicates that you are interested in the individual.

First and last impressions.

The first and last five minutes of the interview are the most important to the interview. It is during this time that critical first and lasting impressions are made and the interviewer decides whether or not you are a viable candidate. Communicate positive behaviours during the first five minutes and be sure you are remembered when you leave.

Remember that the purpose of every interview is to get an offer.

You must sufficiently impress your interviewer both professionally and personally, to be offered the job. At the end of the interview, make sure you know what the next step is and when the employer expects to make a decision.

Understand employers' needs.

Present yourself as someone who can really add value to an organisation. Show that you can fit into the work environment.

Be likeable.

Be enthusiastic. People love to hire individuals who are easy to get along with and who are excited about their company. Be professional. Demonstrate your interest.

Make sure you have the right skills.

Know your competition. How do you compare with your peers in education, experience, training, salary, and career progression? Mention the things you know how to do really well. They are the keys to your next job.

Display an ability to work hard in order to pursue an organisation's goals.

Assume that most interviewers need to select someone who will fit well into their organisation in terms of both productivity and personality. You must confirm that you are both a productive and personable individual by emphasizing the benefits you will bring to the company.

Market all of your strengths.

It is important to market yourself, including your technical qualifications, general skills and experiences as well as personal traits. Recruiters care about two things-credentials and personality. Can you do the job based on past performance and will you fit in with the corporate culture? Talk about your positive personality traits and give examples of how you demonstrate each one on the job.

Give definitive answers and specific results.

Whenever you make a claim of your accomplishments, it will be more believable and better remembered if you cite specific examples and support for your claims.

Tell the interviewer about business situations where you successfully used a skill and elaborate on the outcome. Be specific.

Do not be afraid to admit mistakes.

Employers want to know what mistakes you have made and how you have learned from them. Do not be afraid to admit making mistakes in the past, but continuously stress your positive qualities as well, and how you have turned negatives into positive results.

Relate stories or examples that heighten your past experience.

Past performance is the best indicator of future performance. If you were successful at one company, odds are you can succeed at another. Be ready to sell your skills and performance in the interview.

Know everything about your potential employer before the interview.

Customize your answers as much as possible in terms of the needs of the employer. This requires that you complete research, before the interview, about the company, its customers, and the work you anticipate doing. Talk in the employer's language.

Rehearse and practice interview questions before the interview.

Prior to your interview, try to anticipate the types of questions you may be asked and rehearse the appropriate answers. Even if you do not anticipate all of the questions, the process of thinking them through will help reduce anxiety and be prepared during the interview itself.

Know how to respond to tough questions.

The majority of questions that you will be asked can be anticipated. However, there are exceptional questions tailored to throw you off guard to see how you perform under pressure. Your best strategy is to be prepared, stay calm, collect your thoughts, and respond as clearly as possible.

Aim your strengths, accomplishments and contributions

Use job-related language relevant to the needs of employers. While you no doubt have specific strengths and skills related to the position, emphasise the benefits, you are likely to provide to the employer. Whenever possible, give examples of your strengths that relate to the employer using the appropriate language for the industry.

Identify your strengths and what you enjoy doing.

Skills that you enjoy are the ones that are most likely to bring benefit to an employer. Before the interview, know what it is that you enjoy doing most, and what benefits those skills bring to you and your employer.

Know how you communicate verbally.

Strong verbal communication skills are highly valued by most employers. They are signs of educated and competent individuals. Know how you communicate, and practice with others to determine if you are presenting yourself in the best possible light.

Do not arrive on time-arrive early!

No matter how sympathetic your interviewer may be to the fact that there was an accident on the freeway, it is virtually impossible to overcome a negative first impression. Do whatever it takes to be on time, including allowing extra time for unexpected emergencies.

Treat everyone you meet as important to the interview.

Be courteous to everyone you come in contact with, no matter who they are or what their position. The opinion of everyone can be important to interview success. That includes the receptionist!

The 5-Rule Interview Plan

Still worried about that interview – here are five rules to help you out.

Rule 1: Positive At All Times

The first rule of being a successful interviewee is to be positive at all times. The interviewee must be especially positive about his or her achievements. Direct questions asking a candidate to reveal his shortcomings should not be answered. There are two schools of thought. The first suggests a shortcoming should be turned to advantage thus: -

Candidate: If you must know, my time keeping is dreadful.
Interviewer: How bad is dreadful?

Candidate: I am never in before 8.00 am.
Interviewer: But we do not start until 9.00 am.

Candidate: Well I always aim to be in by quarter-to-eight to give me a full hour before the others start arriving, but I never seem to make it before eight.

Did I hear a groan? That is why I prefer the alternative response of complete denial.

Candidate: I know you will forgive me for not answering this question. To do so would be like me joining your company and then deliberately revealing shortcomings in our company's products.

Occasionally a smart interviewer will describe negative conditions and/or heavy demands upon employees to test a candidate's commitment. The rule again is to be positive regardless. All too often, the picture can be painted much blacker than in reality, but a negative response will soon see that candidate out of the running. I still fondly remember being especially positive about an organisation some years ago – the company was apparently so impressed that this was their justification for not offering me the original post but a different appointment a higher level in their organisation.

Rule 2: Quantitative v Qualitative

The second rule follows directly from the first. To be positive and to make positive claims about one's achievements is simply not enough. Stories about being very popular, about being especially trusted, about being a good timekeeper, are just that – stories. They are best described as providing qualitative information, they are matters of opinion, and they are merely claims.

Therefore, provide as much quantitative information as possible. It is quantitative information which I s often lacking in a C.V. which restricts itself to saying what the individual was responsible for. By quantifying information, it seems that the interviewer will accept its veracity without as much as a raised eyebrow.

Candidates who talk about being promoted within only *x months* a company record, who were always one of the three top performing salesmen, who exceeded sales targets consistently by *y%*, reduced staff turnover a half, completed projects under budget by *x hundred thousand pounds*.

These are the types of descriptions of past performances that bring immediate comfort and reassurance to the interviewer. So satisfying can such quantitative information be that in practice it is only very rarely questioned, or deemed to require further supporting evidence.

Rule 3: No Misunderstandings

It is not enough to be positive; to quantify ones past performances and to ensure that what is said has also been understood. The fourth rule is to ensure that every answer is accepted. This is vital. If the interviewer disagrees with the answer, he is also disagreeing with you as a candidate.

Checking regularly for acceptance is the most important rule of all. It is also very simple to apply. Such intermittent phrases as: Does that cover your question? Does that make sense? How do you feel about that? Would that fit in with your current thinking? Help greatly to change an interrogation into a natural and infinitely more endurable dialogue.

However, more than this, they give the candidate the opportunity to determine if he has said sufficient or whether he needs to expand his point yet further. They are, by this device, also able to elicit the interviewer's approval and to reinforce this process throughout the meeting. We all use jargon. We all forget too easily that such everyday words and phrases in one job are not used universally.

Rule 4: Keeping To The Point

The fourth rule is important both because interviews are of finite length and because a great many interviewers are less than accomplished in managing the interview process.

A question like "What do you think of flexi time?" is so ambiguous in its purpose that no well-prepared candidate will attempt to answer.

Rather than waste five valuable minutes discussing from a management perspective the issues involved in maintaining discipline and productivity in a flexi time environment when, as it turns out, the interviewer was merely interested to know if the candidate would like to work flexible hours himself, the application of the fourth rule becomes essential.

This states that no response should be given until the interviewee is confident that he knows what the interviewer is asking. A simple "That's a big subject, which aspect of it would you like me to address first?" will do the trick.

Rule 5: Be Positive

There seems to be a correlation between the need to emphasise the fifth and final rule and the seniority of the post in question. The interviewee should regularly express his positive attitude toward the employer and the career prospects that it appears to offer.

Candidates seem to feel that declaring an interest in a position, particularly if they have been approached rather than applied, will utterly destroy their bargaining position. Agreeing with such a philosophy would be to encourage an angler to land his hook regardless of whether or not it has a fish affixed to it.

The candidate has no initiative in the matter until the client has not only expressed an intention to make an offer but has actually made it. Then, and only then, when the employer is metaphorically on the hook, does the initiative pass to the candidate who may accept the job offer, refuse it or elect to commence negotiations. However, the more committed to the employer he has been hitherto in the interview, the more comfort will be felt by the employer and the greater the willingness to negotiate.

There is so much that can be said about correct dress, properly researching an employer before interview, and your C.V. However, the above five rules may not be quite so obvious to the average candidate and there is plenty of evidence to show that adherents can immediately become transformed into exceptional candidates.

The Day of the Interview

Well you've done it – you've got the interview, you've done your preparation so now what happens?

Self-confidence sells

Make an effort with your appearance so that you feel good but avoid over dramatic statements. Unless you are applying for a job as a croupier or dancer, heavy make-up, dangling earrings and clanking bangles are distracting. So are loud ties and suits.

Body language

This is hard to change overnight but there are some obvious tips. Remember to keep eye contact, sit forward and try to keep arms and legs uncrossed. Leaning back, with arms folded, staring at the floor looks defensive.

On the day

Take your crib sheet with you, along with a copy of your application, C.V., the job ad and any job description. If you know you make a nervous candidate, try to learn ways of coming across better and refuse the offer of tea or coffee – shaky hands are a dead give-away. Do not leave everything to the interviewer. Early impressions are important and a late flourish of intelligent good points is no good. Equally taking over the interview will not make you popular.

Focus what you want to say on what is relevant to the job. "It is really surprising how often candidate look totally blank when asked how well they think they match the profile for the job. It is as if they saw no need even to think about their skills in relation to those looked for in the successful candidate.

One-to-one interviews have been shown to be more productive and are easier to control, but panel interviews are still the norm. Make sure you listen to the introductions and know each interviewer's special area of interest.

Listen to the questions carefully and use each one as an opportunity to get your point across at the same time as answering the question.

Real life examples are far better than waffle

Interviewers like to pose questions about how you would deal with certain tasks or problems, such as prioritizing a sudden heavy workload or motivating a junior colleague. Try giving a short answer to the specific question but lead on to give an account of what you did in a similar situation in your present or previous job. Keep it short. If you have spoken non-stop for more than five minutes without anyone else getting a look in, it is best to stop.

Try to judge reactions to your answer. If the interviewers are looking down at their notes rather than at you, you may have missed the point.

Do not be afraid to put them on the spot. Try saying: "Does that answer your question?" This way you get another shot at it.

How to say goodbye

Whether things have gone well or badly, after you have had your turn at question time, end on a high note. Take the initiative in saying pleasant things about the interview and finding out how soon you can expect to hear an outcome. If you still want to hear an outcome. If you still want the job, do not forget to say so.

If you do not get the job.

Never mind. Remember, you would not have been selected for an interview if the company did not think you could be the right person. Think about how you could have run the interview differently and put this into practice next time. If you thought it went well but get a rejection, ring up and ask if there is anything particular you could improve on. This is especially worth doing if you are trying to break into a particular career route. Everyone gets turned down sometimes, even the boss. What matters most is that you come away from an interview feeling that you did not let yourself down. Then you have kept the confidence to do even better next time.

Preparing Employer Questions

Yo ou should always have a few questions prepared to ask the employer. They show that you are interested in the company and that you are organised and prepared. There are four rules to follow in preparing your questions for the interviewer.

First: you really care about the topic. If you do not care, do not ask.

Second: your questions reflect the fact that you have read about and have thought about the subject and your question flows from that.

Third: do not let your questions raise doubts or barriers to being hired. For example, do not ask a question like, "Is weekend work necessary?" or "Will I have to travel a lot?" Phrased that way the question makes it seem that you will not be available for weekends or that you do not want to travel and that could pose a problem.

Leave that issue for the interviewer to ask you. What kinds of questions could you ask? Well, you certainly want to ask about the job itself. Who would you be working with? What does it take to be successful?

You may want to ask questions about the company. You might say, "I read in the newspaper that this company's main product has been such and such." Ask a question which follows from that.

You might want to ask a question about the industry or the profession. It is important that the employer knows you see your job in a larger context.

Fourth: you might want to ask about external influences. There are many factors outside of the company and industry that would affect both the company and your job. For example, government policies, the state of the international economy - influences that will affect you even though you cannot control them.

Five Questions They'll Love...

I n case you are stumped with your questions here are a few suggestions.

Ask them to describe their ideal candidate for the job. If they mention experience or skills, you have not had the chance to talk about, talk about them now.

If not already covered, **ask about development and training opportunities.** How can you progress with the company? Are there any relevant qualifications you should think about getting? If so, does the company help with studying for these?

If it is a team role, **ask about the skills and experience of other team members**, but not what they are like.

Try to ask **something relevant about the company** to show that you have taken an interest in more than just the job.

Ask the interviewer what they most enjoy about their job and what makes it exciting for them. This will help you judge whether the company is right for you.

And Five They will Hate!

Here are the ones that your should NOT ask....

Do not ask **about pay, hours of work, holidays or perks.** You should have this information already, but if not, ask about these things when offered the job and before accepting it.

Do not ask **why the last person left the job**. Asked as a direct question it will not gain you any useful information and may mark you out as trouble

Do not **ask for your expenses** if these have not been offered. The policy on expenses should have been clear in the invitation to the interview.

Do not set **any conditions on when you need to hear** if you do have deadlines on other offers, ring up the next day to discuss this.

Do **not ask whether you have the job.** Question time is still part of the interview and few people like to give instant feedback.

Job Offers

Now that I have a new job, is my job search over?

You've thought over your new job offer and decided to accept it. Does that mean that your job search is over? Well, not really.

- First, it is important to remember all those people who helped you get this job offer. Let them know that you've accepted the position and thank them for all the help they gave you.

- Secondly, you may still have many years ahead of you in your career. If so, it is important to make a list of those things you need to do in the new job to make sure you're successful at it. And think one-step ahead, whether you remain with this employer or go to another employer, you will be looking for new experiences and challenges in your career. Think about those things you could be doing on the new job, which will help you prepare for the next one.

Evaluating Your Job Offer

Congratulations! Someone has offered you a new job opportunity. Should you accept it? The first thing to do is ask yourself, "What do I really want in my next job?" Then take that whole list of things you want and rank order them. What is the most important, second most, and so forth? Once you have made a list of what you want from your next job, you can compare that to what you expect to gain from the offer.

If most of what you want is going to be met, you should seriously be considering saying yes. If you find that there are some things important to you that are lacking you should seriously be thinking about giving a polite no.

Follow Up Visits

When a new job has been offered to you, I strongly encourage you to visit the firm for a follow-up visit. That is, I suggest that you spend at least one day at the firm, watching people work, seeing how they relate to each other, getting a sense of the atmosphere.

It is true that you have been to the company before for the interview process, but then you were nervous and tense and you were trying to sell yourself. At a follow-up visit, you can make observations and ask about things that may not have occurred to you before. That way you can confirm or question your initial impressions of the company.

Secondly, peace of mind is very important. When you make a decision, you want to know that you have taken into account everything you reasonably could know about the job, about the company, about your own feelings of comfort or discomfort with that situation. By making the follow-up visit, you will know that everything you could possibly learn about that company, you have learned.

Negotiating Your Salary Package

Congratulations. A new job has been offered to you. Perhaps you want to negotiate for a higher salary. Here are some steps to follow:

First, make sure that you really want the job. If you do, you can say to the employer, "I really want this job, I like the job, the company, the people I'd be working with - there is only one thing that's making me hesitate to say yes, and that's the salary. If you could offer me, let's say five thousand dollars more, I'd say yes right now."

Secondly, make sure you understand an employer's basis for agreeing to added compensation. It is not about family needs or things you want to buy - the basis is your value to the company. I recommend that negotiations of this kind be conducted face to face. It is much easier for an employer to say yes under those circumstances.

Who should bring up salary?

It is in your best interest to have the employer bring up a salary figure or range first, and then discuss it in person, or at least over the phone.

When should a salary discussion start?

Salary negotiation should only begin after you have demonstrated how your skills, education, experience; accomplishments qualify you as the best candidate for the position.

What other benefits should I ask for?

Salary is not the only important component of an overall compensation package. There are many other benefits that you should consider including medical, eye-care and dental coverage, vacation, car allowances, profit sharing programs, pension contribution, stock option plans and many more. It is always a good idea to ask about the company's benefits programme.

Action Phrases and Power Verbs

Describing your work experience isn't easy. To help you, we have compiled a list of action phrases and power verbs. The purpose of using them is to show employers that you know how to get results. Begin your job descriptions with a power verb or phrase: enlisted the support..., formed a committee..., sold, budgeted, improved, increased, maintained the client relationship.

Action Phrases

Design, develop and deliver; Conduct needs analysis; Write course design documents; Manage development; Consult with clients; Facilitate problem-solving meetings; Implement solutions; Develop and implement formatting; Developed and delivered;

Revamped product training; Assessed employee and client training needs; Analyzed evaluation data; Designed and implemented; followed special task force; assisted special task force; facilitated discussion;

Reduced manufacturing plant's burden; Reduced material costs; Managed an eleven-person team; negotiated over £T/O; Coordinated strategic five-year plan; created and implemented innovative approach; developed new product;

Power Verbs

Accelerated acclimated accompanied accomplished achieved acquired acted activated actuated adapted added addressed adhered adjusted administered admitted adopted advanced advertised advised advocated aided aired affected allocated altered amended amplified analyzed answered anticipated appointed appraised approached approved arbitrated arranged ascertained asked assembled assigned assumed assessed assisted attained attracted audited augmented authored authorized automated awarded avail

Balanced bargained borrowed bought broadened budgeted built

calculated canvassed capitalized captured carried out cast catalogued centralized challenged chaired changed channelled charted checked chose circulated clarified classified cleared closed co-authored cold called collaborated collected combined commissioned committed communicated compared compiled complied completed composed computed conceived conceptualized concluded condensed conducted conferred consolidated constructed consulted contracted contrasted contributed contrived controlled converted convinced co-ordinated corrected corresponded counselled counted created critiqued cultivated cut

Debugged decided decentralized decreased deferred defined delegated delivered demonstrated depreciated described designated designed determined developed devised devoted diagrammed directed disclosed discounted discovered dispatched displayed dissembled distinguished distributed diversified divested documented doubled drafted

Earned eased edited effected elected eliminated employed enabled encouraged endorsed enforced engaged engineered enhanced enlarged enriched entered entertained established estimated evaluated examined exceeded exchanged executed exempted exercised expanded expedited explained exposed extended extracted extrapolated

Facilitated familiarized fashioned fielded figured financed fit focused forecasted formalized formed formulated fortified found founded framed fulfilled functioned

Gained gathered gauged gave generated governed graded granted greeted grouped guided handled headed hired hosted

Identified illustrated illuminated implemented improved improvised inaugurated indoctrinated increased incurred induced influenced informed initiated innovated inquired inspected inspired installed instigated instilled instituted instructed insured interfaced interpreted interviewed introduced invented inventoried invested investigated invited involved isolated issued

Joined judged

Launched lectured led lightened liquidated litigated lobbied localized located

Maintained managed mapped marketed maximized measured mediated merchandised merged met minimized modelled moderated modernized modified monitored motivated moved multiplied

Named narrated negotiated noticed nurtured

Observed obtained offered offset opened operated orchestrated ordered organised oriented originated overhauled oversaw

Paid participated passed patterned penalized perceived performed permitted persuaded phased out pinpointed pioneered placed planned polled prepared presented preserved presided prevented priced printed prioritized probed processed procured produced profiled programmed projected promoted prompted proposed proved provided publicized published purchased pursued

Quantified quoted

Raised ranked rated reacted read received recommended reconciled recorded recovered recruited rectified redesigned reduced referred refined regained regulated rehabilitated reinforced reinstated rejected related remedied remodelled renegotiated reorganised replaced repaired reported represented requested researched resolved responded restored restructured resulted retained retrieved revamped revealed reversed reviewed revised revitalized rewarded routed

Safeguarded salvaged saved scheduled screened secured segmented selected sent separated served serviced settled shaped shortened showed shrank signed simplified sold solved spearheaded specified speculated spoke spread stabilized staffed staged standardized steered stimulated strategize streamlined strengthened stressed structured studied submitted substantiated substituted suggested summarized superseded supervised supplied supported surpassed surveyed synchronized synthesized systematized

Tabulated tailored targeted taught terminated tested testified tightened took traced traded trained transacted transferred transformed translated transported travelled treated tripled

Uncovered undertook unified united updated upgraded used utilized

Validated valued verified viewed visited

Weighed welcomed widened witnessed won worked wrote

Brought to You By The Biz Guru

"If you need help with your business – click or brick – we're here to help"

www.BizGuruServices.com

www.JobSuccess.co.uk

www.ResumeGuys.com

Index:

A

achievements · 16, 18, 23, 24, 51, 52, 55, 56, 108, 109

Action Phrases · 126

Applying Online · 83

artistic role · 25

B

Biz Guru Ltd. · 10

Body language · 114

C

Career · 16, 17, 18, 20, 23, 52, 74

Career Experience · 16, 17, 23

Career Objective · 17, 18

Career Overview · 16, 20

Changing Careers · 43

Chronological CV · 16

Company Application · 34

Cover Letter · 28, 40

crib sheet · 93, 114

CV Blunders · 58

CV Check List · 29

CV Writing Errors · 49

D

Design of Your CV · 24

E

employment security · 75

Ethical Issues · 80

F

Functional CV · 16, 17, 52

future employer · 31, 84

G

Gaps in Work History · 42

graduate · 12, 58

Graduate · 15, 45

Grammar · 30, 58

H

Headers and Footers · 19

I

interview · 12, 20, 22, 30, 41, 43, 44, 47, 48, 50, 51, 58, 60, 80, 92, 93, 94, 96, 97, 98, 100, 101, 102, 103, 105, 106, 107, 108, 111, 113, 114, 116, 120, 122

Interview Plan · 108

Interview Preparation · 92

Interview Strategy · 13

Interview Techniques · 91

Interview Tips · 102

interviewer's questions · 99

IT role · 22

IT Staff · 33

J

Job Offers · 121

Job Search Plan · 89

Job Searching Strategies · 68

Job Searching Strategy · 13

K

Key Achievements · 17, 23

Key Skills · 17, 24

L

languages · 22

Legal Notice · 10

M

Medical · 34

N

Negatives in your Work History · 44

Networking · 76

New Graduates · 33

O

Out of Work · 42

Over Qualified · 47

P

Personal Achievements · 18, 24
Personal Statement · 20
Power Verbs · 126, 127
professor · 22
Professor · 15
Professors · 34
proper dress · 98
publications · 22, 52, 90

Q

Qualifications · 16, 17, 18, 21, 59

R

Recent Graduates · 32
References · 53
Relevant Experience · 18, 24
research · 22, 32, 78, 90, 98, 105
right skills · 104
risk · 10

S

Salary · 124, 125
Sales Staff · 33
Self Marketing · 78
Senior Manager · 33
spelling · 29, 30, 41
Structure Of Your CV · 49
Student CV · 18
Students · 32, 36

T

Technical Skills · 22
Technology · 81, 82
Tips On Writing Your CV · 30
To Do List, · 13

U

unemployed · 12, 54

V

verb phrases · 32
vocational guidance tests · 71

W

Web Personae · 84

www.jobsuccess.co.uk · 12

www.JobSuccess.co.uk · 4, 70, 79, 131

www.ResumeGuys.com · 70, 79, 131

www.ingramcontent.com/pod-product-compliance
Lightning Source LLC
Chambersburg PA
CBHW022059210326
41518CB00038B/299